D1591574

DISCARD

AMONGST
IMMORTALS RAGING

AMONGST IMMORTALS RAGING

Gettysburg's Third Day Begins

MARSHALL CONYERS

PELICAN PUBLISHING COMPANY
GRETNA 2007

*The word "Pelican" and the depiction of a pelican
are trademarks of Pelican Publishing Company, Inc.,
and are registered in the U.S. Patent and Trademark Office.*

Library of Congress Cataloging-in-Publication Data

Conyers, Marshall.
    Amongst immortals raging : Gettysburg's third day begins / Marshall
Conyers.
        p. cm.
    ISBN 978-1-58980-468-5 (alk. paper)
    1. Gettysburg, Battle of, Gettysburg, Pa., 1863—Poetry. 2. War poetry,
American. 3. Historical poetry, American. I. Title.
    PS3603.O5674A83 2007
    811'.6—dc22

                                                                              2007005788

Printed in the United States of America

Published by Pelican Publishing Company, Inc.
1000 Burmaster Street, Gretna, Louisiana 70053

For my mama and daddy,
who sleep forever now with angels

Of blood and honor . . . death and glory

CONTENTS

★ ★ ★ ★

The Gray   11

Transition   53

The Blue   59

Retreat   93

Aftermath   99

Requiem   107

Acknowledgments   111

AMONGST
IMMORTALS RAGING

THE GRAY

★ ★ ★ ★

Army of Northern Virginia
JULY 3, 1863

Gen. Robert E. Lee

★ ★ ★ ★

standing just outside headquarters

5:02 A.M.

Unlimbering, *the Mighty Beast awakes,*
sensing, seeking this day's blood.
Men, *mere boys,*
resolved by dawn's gray unresolving light,
rise, murmur, move,
shadow wraiths cast against
the failing depths of night.
The hush, the muffled groan of early camp arousal
mark an army gaining greater volume
as a thousand fires wink on.
Impressive, grandly *lethal* in the twining mists of dawn,
but *clamorous* now,
more robust with the gaining light,
the vastness of our northern march
defines itself against the gentle swelling hills
and fields of ripening summer corn.

Close by, a Whip-o-will sings its last sweet song of night.
An omen of some kind? Perhaps.
I do not know for sure . . .

    . . . but today, it's all come down to this.

I stand upon this distant July place
peering out uneasy at the quickening hills
for sleep has found me lacking in the night
and unbound the doubt in me.
To what desperate end this day will come, I cannot say,
beyond my devotion to those who've followed me over glory
to a final resolution here.

All of it . . . *our* land . . . the very *Cause* itself,
each of us bound by brief mortality one to each other,
all of it, I've staked upon the boldness of this thrust. . . .

    . . . Dear God, how I love these magnificent Southern boys!

To Duty's clarion call,
they answered uncomplaining,
beneath bright banners waving
marched off to "Dixie" playing . . .
dirt farmers, mostly, who've never been
even ten short miles from home . . .
boys who bleed their innocence so freely
just to earn the sole proprietary right to die
like fighting men . . .
so gentle,
so serene,
yet, made over into instruments so terribly fierce
since this awful cataclysm swept them up and in.

Now, full light comes at last.
Day breaks brighter slanting in
striking gold amidst mid-summer trees,
mules bray rancorous, far and near,
cannon creak and clank and roll,
men form up in ranks and rows.
With heat, the mists of summer lift
to twirl and twine away.
A vast gray tide reveals itself more starkly now,
about to *roar* and *break.*

I sense this *place,* this very *day,*
the brutalness to come,
as somehow pivotal of a *moment* in our time.
Off it, many things will turn.

I gaze more fully out upon the beauty of the scene,
upon the beast unlimbered, fully *roused,*
soon to be unleashed.
Now, I ask the *driving question,*
not of any living creature other than
my Creator and myself . . .

   . . . has any one man ever wielded such an awesomely destructive weapon
with so much absolute regret?

I think not
I *know* not
but always, I justify the horribly vexing question
with three small cherished words . . .

Duty   Honor   Country

yet, truly, in the end,
it all comes down to love . . .
love of these gentle Southern boys,
fierce warriors one and all,
bound by blood and horror,
by perfect glory too . . .
brothers who love each other dearly
and me too,
who would gladly die for me and do . . .
which makes the extreme weight of my decision
taken here today
the greater over all.

   "General," a voice approaches, calls out familiarly from behind.

I turn about.
George Pickett stands there grinning in the dappled morning light.
Pickett . . . the epitome of all boldness,
high embodied essence of the glory of command.

   "General Lee," his words leap through his boyish grin, "the sun is up.
   I feel great things in store for us today. I am at your service, sir."

Feigning certainty, I reply,

   "You are right, General. Perhaps you can take the field by noon?"

   "I can, indeed, sir. My division stands ready at your command."

In a moment, he is gone.
Behind him now lingers a trace of romantic glory,
the quintessential warrior essence which constitutes the man.
Pickett . . . with him goes all that *we* are,
all that our new land ever hopes to be.

But the problem still remains:
that one little ridge looming a mile or so away.

I turn my attention full upon it now,
and once more onto *Pickett,*
history's lone transitional figure,
a gallant cavalier,

striding old times and the new.
If *anyone* can do it, Pickett can.

The decision *made.*
The moment *done.*
Our fate, I give over into God's eternal hands.

Lt. Gen. James Longstreet

★ ★ ★ ★

pacing inside his tent

5:27 A.M.

Sleep never optioned me this night,
has not come,
nor will it ever so easily again
now that *the moment* draws so nearly down upon us.

Caged by early morning's light,
I pace the shadowed confines of my tent
convinced by restlessness
and the simple logic of my eyes
of the tragic folly of it all.
Quietly, I pose the single question
painfully obvious to any other than the blind . . .

    . . . can no one see the terrible bloodbath soon to come?

Rhetorically, I must answer to the plainly obvious:
Dear God in heaven, no!
no one sees, at least
until the battle's finally joined
to the wasted detriment of our proud legions
caught up in death's benumbing thrall.

Truly, I love *him,*
never questioned that at all,
love him so very dearly . . .
Godlike almost in his affinity for us all . . .
I've watched him suffer tragedy unbearable,
seen his heart ache sorely, too,
felt his growing sadness,
admired his flair for genius,
up 'til now,
when needed least of all,
his wrongly held belief in *invincibility*
soon to unhinge hell's floodgates
and sweep us all away
in a fury of violence and of blood.

Madness . . . sheer madness,
those waiting heights,
impregnable with cannon, men, and guns . . .
but still, he thinks our boys can do it,
cross that mile-long gently rising sward
beneath death's deadly promenade,
as though Providence itself wills him to
commit this act of folly, strategic and supreme.

Alone, in our war council late of just last night,
I stated flatly my objections, saying,

> "Sir, I do not believe those heights can be taken.
> Nay, I *know* they cannot be taken."

Dead silence
amidst my words of hanging lead,
issued formally,
suspended cold upon the hot tent air,
pole lanterns sharply flickering,
casting giant tent shadows,
each thrown out and oddly holding
history's single greatest general transfixed
in frozen shadow-shape relief . . .

. . . until he spoke up in his gentle unassuming way. . . .

> "It is my belief that those heights can be taken, General . . .
> that they *will* be taken by sometime late tomorrow afternoon."

And that was all.
I subsided,
nodding.

Yet, still another more vexing question looms
to which I alone must affix a soldier's answer . . .

> . . . *wherein lies my supreme duty in this matter?*

Advising staunchly against this charge,
yes, I've surely done indeed.
Yet the legitimate parameters of my command,
I've not pushed beyond one whit at all,
and still, I wonder,
should I?
Should I perhaps *resign?*

Truly, the thought has crossed my mind,
roundly to be dismissed by the obedient soldier I remain.

My obedience weighed against the death of thousands . . .
an awful weight to forever bear alone.

I step outside my tent.
The army well awake,
brisk at work among the
summer smells of earth and early morning air.

Ah . . . but here comes Pickett now,
grinning pure sunlight among the trees.
Poor sad fierce warrior boy,
fame will surely coin his name,
grant gallantry its rightful due
beyond the briefness of this day
and the tragedy inevitably to come.

★ ★ ★ ★

Maj. Gen. George Pickett

★ ★ ★ ★

approaching through the trees

5:31 A.M.

Early dawn . . .
day wars indecisively with night,
that period indistinguishable,
as substanceless as fog,
yet, the air so sweet, so soft,
perfumed by a thousand earthy smells.

I stride invigorated by it all,
the hour
the moment here
our victory soon to come,
'til *there,*
just up ahead outside his soldier's tent,
I see among the semi-trees
now gaining with the rush to light,
Longstreet,
standing sturdy as a strong old oak himself.

   "Good morning, sir."

I speak formally once,
then stop dead *still,*
regarding of the pale dour face,
the brooding eyes,
where something *strange* has come to rest,
as cold as doubt itself,
a look beyond *foreboding.*

   "Good morning, George."

his reply comes pleasantly enough,
though his words seem oddly forced,
which gives me pause to press on more forthrightly.

   "Are you feeling all right, sir?" I ask.

   "Yes," he speaks softly once.

Yet, within his single word of quick reply,
there is *dismissal,*
and what I swear is surely *sadness,* too.

But who could possibly deal in sadness
on this oh so glorious day?

So, I salute,
pass on smiling brightly on this early summer morn
elated
intoxicated
my division lethally positioned as a perfect extension of myself,
listening for the horns of victory
to sound forth *my* magnificent charge.

Truly, I am beloved of God,
chosen as His single instrument of deliverance.
I, once so roundly taunted at The Point,
. . . *they* all called *me* dumb . . .
whose division now readies to strike history's profoundest blow.

Yes
me
George Pickett
chosen by our beloved commander
to lead us on the coming day
'til victory's halls,
its hallowed places,
re-echo with the sounding of my name:
Pickett.

A Whip-o-will sings close by at hand,
a good omen, I suspect,
and there stands Pettigrew not too very far away.

> "General," I pause to say, "how do you see things
> on the day?"

Pettigrew stares out and up across the gently rising way,
calculates momentarily, then replies,

> "You'll command those heights by sometime
> late this afternoon, General."

Pettigrew . . . a good man from Carolina, very dependable.
I move on, thinking wryly . . .

Yes, those heights are mine,
then shortly later on,
all fame and glory too.

★ ★ ★ ★

Brig. Gen. James Pettigrew

★ ★ ★ ★

staring up at the heights

5:49 A.M.

Those distant heights:
too much
too far away
too many heavy Yankee guns
and poor misguided *Pickett,*
knight errantry's proud romantic son
who, Quixotic-like, embodies the warrior's myth,
the living legend of *himself* with still yet no battle won.

But this day, glory's blind spot
will offer up the perfect sacrifice:
Pickett
valiant self-enamored fool.
God help us all,
butchery awaits,
though I won't admit it much beyond myself . . .

. . . and what of Trimble now?
off there so hurried,
so swiftly passing by.
Obedient soldier that he is in every single way,
yet, still I pause to wonder:
does he feel it pretty much as I?
sense the scale of tragedy fast approaching
on this last and fateful day?

★ ★ ★ ★

Maj. Gen. Isaac Trimble

★ ★ ★ ★

on his way to the latrine

5:58 A.M.

If not for Ewell's colossal stupidity,
if not for his blind-eyed blundering strategic idiocy

    . . . damn him!

we would hold the higher ground this day,
be dug in even now,
positioned there to strike them well,
to deal out disproportionate death,
rather than ill disposed within this purgatory place
from which we'll all too soon march up and out
straight into raging Yankee hell.

Please,
if *You* are listening,
forgive my blaspheming words,
for I am *very* troubled in my soul . . .

. . . me, poor Isaac Trimble, your faithful servant,
a very religious man, yes, I truly am indeed,
who dwells at length upon the opportunities
missed upon that first most fateful day.
Yes, I, your humble servant who . . .

    . . . by the lifelong devoutness of my Christian faith
    do hereby once again reaffirm the power of that dreadful curse
    I previously laid on Dick Ewell's empty head

        . . . damn him!!

Father, forgive me, please.
Your heavenly pardon, I beg once more,
for I have said *it* once again.

★ ★ ★ ★

Lt. Gen. Richard Ewell

★ ★ ★ ★

seated . . . loading his pistol

6:09 A.M.

I am the sole . . . the solitary architect of *this,*
this hour all encompassing
and all too soon to come.
I *alone*
who spun this needless soldier's web,
who fashioned it with brooding,
now soon to drip with noble Southern blood.

Dick Ewell . . .
long to be remembered for what I never did,
who did not *act* when action called,
who owned those heights
for the simple taking,
yet, who *froze,*
immobilized with indecision
chiseled to the very marrow of my bones.

Poor Trimble
begged,
he *pleaded,*
raged finally out at last . . .

> *For God's sake, take that hill! he cried.*

I could not budge,
glued there,
rooted to the spot.

And Trimble,
beside himself, exasperated,
cried out once again . . .

> *I'll take it then . . . just give me a division.*

I could not speak.

> *Give me a brigade, he pleaded.*

I could not speak.

Give me a regiment, he roared straight out at last.

and still I could not speak.

Old Isaac Trimble, good soldier that he is,
damns me roundly in his heart, I know,
yet, if we win here on the day,
all is well again.

Lord, I beg of thee . . . please . . . let us win here on the day.

★ ★ ★ ★

J. S. B. Cullen

★ ★ ★ ★

surgeon—Longstreet's Corps

6:44 A.M.

Winning?
Losing?

Thoughts of neither hold my tools of trade,
draw no such sharp distinctions.

So, sharpen up my *cutter's* blade,
hone the toothy hacking saws for battle's time to come,
to slice my way through blood and bone,
a *slaughterhouse* of sounds,
amid the roaring tide of *shrieks,*
amongst the awful *moans.*

Once finished,
my healer's hands will surely shake to tremble
. . . *healer's hands?* . . .
a damned good joke
that gives me pause to think . . .

> . . . *soon as this Godforsaken day is finally done,*
> *I'll need more than just one drink.*

★ ★ ★ ★

Abner Applewhite

★ ★ ★ ★

fourteen years old—drummer boy—Pickett's Division

6:45 A.M.

My best friend, Cory, and I
were drinking coffee 'round our fire . . .

. . . when our company's first lieutenant
stepped within its tiny glow,
stared down at us, and said,

> "Boys, there's a big battle coming on the day.
> Our orders are to take those distant heights up there."

He pointed off then, far away,
then added as he turned about to leave,

> "And when the hour is come full upon us, I know you'll
> both stand tall and make our company proud."

Yes,
but those heights are highly fortified,
I was thinking quietly to myself,
when Cory suddenly voiced my thoughts aloud.

> "I never expected to live to be full-growed anyhow,"
> he said. "You scared, Abner?"

> "Hell, yes, I'm scared."

> "Your mama could hear you cussin' like a man she'd
> wash your mouth with soap."

Mama,
who I'll probably never see again
because of that long valley rising gently up
to that distant ridgeline bristling
with heavy Yankee guns . . .

. . . then, Cory speaking up matter-of-fact-like once again . . .

> "Today, a lot of good Southern boys are going

to end up very, very dead."

"God help us all," I said.

★ ★ ★ ★

Lee

astride Traveler among the trees, recalling Stuart's
earlier absence and contemplating the battle soon to come

9:00 A.M.

Oh, hear us when we pray to Thee for we are . . .

blind,
without benefit of eyes,
the army stumbles
groping eyeless in the dark,
the beast made sightless of *itself,*
worse than any Polyphemus tortured.

His grand ride around all glory has
left us merely *guessing* at our foe . . .
that *errant* Southern boy . . .

> *. . . where is he . . . where is Jeb Stuart?*

Yet, once more, I beg the question
raised up to Providence now . . .

Father, please,
I need to know
I have to know

> *. . . in heaven's name . . .*
> *where is James Ewell Brown Stuart?*

The *question* largely posed,
yet, answered late of yesterday . . .
the turmoil caused me by his soldier's absence,
the impotence of those first two fighting days,
the anger boiling,
simmering hotly in my aching chest,
resolved at last by Stuart's grand return.

My anger's gone as well,
subsided some,

for he is with us now,
horse-mounted cavalier,
glorious warrior boy,
on this, the third day of our fate . . .

. . . yet, *the eyes* we needed then so desperately,
I fear, may have come back to us
a wee bit just *too late.*

★ ★ ★ ★

Longstreet

★ ★ ★ ★

polishing his boots . . . ruminating on Stuart's earlier absence

9:15 A.M.

. . . Where is Stuart?

Indeed,
the question earlier posed
by many more than once,
brought lights of anger quickly brimming
to our beloved commander's eyes . . .
then, swiftly gone,
the fires blown out to gentler places far away,
transmogrified by sadness
and shrugs of solemn resignation, too.

Damn you, Stuart,
jaunty cavalier with a plume so useless in your hat,
returned so grandly from your cavalry joy ride . . .

. . . not your fierceness called into question now,
for battle's tested you quite well,
nor your personal valor that I would bring
summarily before a court . . .

. . . it's your total lack of *judgment* here
in these final hours teetering crux-like
on the fulcrum of our times.

True son of war,
you have no fighting peer, Jeb Stuart.
Purest warrior that you are,
your likeness will not be seen again
for a thousand years to come.

Yet, be that as it may,
among us, there be those who still wish
to sit in *judgment* of your recent absence . . .

. . . and rightly so, I say.

★ ★ ★ ★

Maj. Gen. J. E. B. Stuart

★ ★ ★ ★

**returning in his thoughts to his ride around
the Army of the Potomac**

9:25 A.M.

*Yesterday,
I recall just how . . .*

. . . a dog barks fiercely as we pass,
yet, the countryside remains at rest,
at ease,
merely curious at best.

Citizens stand unarmed before their doors,
line long front porches too,
and simply *stare* . . .
old farmers mostly, stolid types,
their wives, careworn with age and *us* . . .
a few young girls, they sadly smile;
the prettiest
coyly choose to lift their hands and wave.

My boys respond,
high gentlemen of The South,
its finest flower,
youth with deadly potency combined,
cantering . . .
so terribly proud,
sunlight striking fire to sabers sheathed,
we cut a gallant soldier's sight,
riding . . .
our cavalry,
bold horse legions clad in noble gray,
riding ever on to glory
'round the impotent body of our foe.

    Yet, ever capricious are The Wayward Fates,
    the threads that bind us to our times.
    Today all talk is not of glory . . .

             . . . today I stand accused.

★ ★ ★ ★

Stuart

★ ★ ★ ★

**riding at the head of his mounted legion . . . brooding
over his July 2 meeting with Lee**

10:15 A.M.

I will not live so long enough to heal
this cut unwounded deep in me . . .
saber-like
it bleeds,
condemnation beaming from his saddened eyes.

    I let him down . . .

. . . our beloved commander
addressing me alone,
his words voiceless almost on the evening air,
so soft,
so terribly *still* . . .
he spoke there solemn on the hour,
in the failing light of day,
not forgiving of my historic ride around all glory,
just resigned to the glaring error of my ways.

I did not even *know* I erred,
yet, I offered him my sword,
but *no,* he waved me off. . . .

    "We have no time for that," he said.

★ ★ ★ ★

Brig. Gen. Lewis Armistead

★ ★ ★ ★

sitting on a stump by the wood line, thinking of Winfield Hancock

12:00 P.M.

An hour before the conflict's to be joined,
consecrated by blood and sacrifice,
I penned this poem just for you,
my dearest old friend, Win.

Brief, it is, and goes like this:

> We both built this ship we sail,
> it has no mast, it needs no rail.
> Undaunted by all stormy gusts,
> it navigates on truth and trust;
> a sturdy ship, it needs no wind,
> this ship we built which we call *"friend."*

I fondly wrote these words of *us,*
looking up to where you stand now
looking straight back down . . .
two old warriors,
dutiful ever to our Cause,
to honor,
to friendship always . . .

. . . yet war's dark killer birds, we also are
perched to slay with talons raised,
death's raptors staring coldly back at each other.

Truly, Win,
if The Reaper's hand is meant
to hold us either on this bitter day,
let it be me, my dear old faithful friend.

Ah . . . but now the call to arms is raised . . .
the beast . . . *our* beast,
massive
lethal
roiling hot with mayhem stirs,

cold-eyed
awake . . .

. . . 15,000 gather on the gently rising sward,
cannon roll to take their volleying place,
drums sound out to strike a cadenced beat . . .

    rat-a-tat-tat . . . rat-a-tat-tat

death's bleak music,
a sterile tune,
played out for killing's sake,
to launch the thunder-boom of earthly guns
that soon will heaven shake.

Win,
life cannot bridge our great divide
except through exigencies of war,
but Death be not half so particular.
Beyond this high moment in our lives,
we will not be separate again.

Goodbye, my dear old faithful friend.
Goodbye,
until we meet again.

★ ★ ★ ★

Ol' Dan

★ ★ ★ ★

a caisson-pulling mule with Porter Alexander's artillery

12:59 P.M.

Faithful?
yes, I surely am indeed,
yet, they're all so certain I cannot *comprehend,*
think much beyond my sterile nose,
beyond the driest foulest fodder I am fed.
The way I stand chewing out my stoic days,
steadfast
methodical
drowsy eyed at rest,
convinces them I'm *dumb . . .*
poor dumb expendable beast
wasted in an excess of their glory and their blood,
my useless braying all but still unheard
amidst the booming death of dying,
amidst the roar of guns.

I protest . . . but cannot shun this fate I did nothing to deserve.
Who will speak for me?
for *us . . .* our sad four-legged kind,
so incapable of making carnage
which so mars the race of *them.*
Stubborn, they call us. Ha!
It is *they,* grim harbingers of *themselves,*
who refuse to learn the simple lessons not to kill.

But my fate is brief and written thus:
to haul,
to pull out the last gasping efforts of my life.
For naught, my voiceless braying
lifts above these violent days
unheard by any ear
except for *Him,*
who made me as I am.

★ ★ ★ ★

Porter Alexander

★ ★ ★ ★

Longstreet's Chief of Artillery

1:00 P.M.

"Shoot!"

> . . . *Boom Boom Boom Boom Ka-Boom Boom Boom*
> *Boom Boom Boom Boom*

Upon my order given,
our great barrage begins . . .
140 guns on line,
heavy cannon firing . . .

> . . . *Ka-Boom Boom Boom Boom Boom Boom Boom Boom* . . .

the *earth* itself relenting,
to momentary shake in space,
to groan with inner trembling,
deafening,
like nothing ever *seen* before,
and still we load to shoot again
and shoot again once more . . .

> . . . *Boom Boom Boom Boom Ka-Boom Boom Boom* . . .

our cannon fire,
leap back in spouting tongues of flame,
these perfect salvos opening
to split the red hot air.

Dark bores,
all-raging *mouths* of iron
speak loud with whistling cannon slugs.
Hell opens up,
its breath of *death* poured coldly forth
upon those distant heights above.

★ ★ ★ ★

Brig. Gen. Richard Garnett

★ ★ ★ ★

astride his horse . . . *waiting*

1:30 P.M.

The order has been issued

 . . . no officer shall ride . . .

yet, my situation's such I cannot walk.

So into battle, I will go,
a *target* mounted among men,
for honor permits no exemption
or *escape* once even slightly tarnished.

Touched vaguely by the smallest disrepute,
one's recourse lies only in Death's End.

In such final lights as these,
I sit my horse this hour,
each breath indrawn-exhaled
weighted by *dishonor's* gravest pallor,
anointed,
tinctured by its noisome odor,
stained,
jaundiced by its bone-bare bleakness.

To Hell's End, my brigade will surely follow
even now beyond its burning gate,
. . . my boys respect me ever as a fighting man . . .
yet, once the *coward's* charge is made,
wrongly becomes irrelevant
because the *accusation* jades,
sticks mortally to one's soul.

Jackson, who called me into question,
God rest him,
perfect warrior that he was,
was not always perfect in his judgments as a man.

But he is gone,

while I remain to ride before my proud brigade,
awaiting that lovely order soon to raise,
to begin our vast assault . . .
wanly smiling just to know,
I'll breathe no more of summer air,
see no more blue sky above . . .

. . . to ask forgiveness of my loved ones now
for I ride off eagerly in search of *Her*.
Beyond this final hour here,
Death's Shield Maiden will carry my sharp lance.

Father,
forgive me,
please,
for I go in search of peace
and absolution now.

★ ★ ★ ★

Abner Applewhite

★ ★ ★ ★

drummer boy—Pickett's Division

2:45 P.M.

Mama . . .

we stand upon this gently rising sward,
our division formed . . . *waiting,*
great gathered blocks of men
tethered all by utter silence,
except for banners snapping softly,
waving brightly on the early July breeze.

Fronting on battalions,
officers stand statuesque in gray,
poised,
swords lowered,
held ever at the ready,
awaiting that *one great order* soon to come.

My drum waits ever at the ready, too,
sticks hovered to strike a cadenced beat,
mindful of this impending moment,
in *all* time itself unbalanced strangely,
hanging primed upon this very instant
as though God Himself cups both conflicting sides
in one huge eternal hand,
about to cast them gently down and say . . .

> *"There . . . now let your little battle rage."*

. . . while not too far behind, my best friend,
Cory, whispers hoarse with fear . . .

> "Them big Yankee guns up there on them heights, Abner,
> just behind that far stone wall . . . they got me sorta worried."

> "Yeah, Cory," I whisper back with trembling, "they got me
> sorta worried, too."

Suddenly, *it* comes,

the brief command . . . *the order* given,
and off we *move* as one,
human pieces bound by heritage and blood
lockstepping forward as a single fighting whole.

Mama,
you would be so proud of me this day.
I pace out front proudly like a man,
my drum beating steady rhythms to a tune . . .

    rat-a-tat-tat . . . rat-a tat-tat

. . . to the greater shuffle-step of measured thousands
moving slowly up death's valley in perfect ranks and rows.

Brothers, *Mama,*
15,000 of *us* . . .
long since, the older men quit teasing,
calling me *just a child,*
we who do not fear to die with General Pickett,
proudly exhorting us one and all . . .

    "Forward, boys, forward!" he shouts out urgently,
    then, more passionately, he roars, *"Now, yell, boys, yell!"*

    . . . *Yaaaiiihhh*

thunderous, it lifts . . .
rolling . . .
rippling down our mighty ranks,
angels avenging with our fearsome throated *yell,*
heard distantly beyond that far stone wall
waiting stoically, patiently up ahead,
muskets bristling there,
shifting slightly in response,
shimmering deadly in the humid July sun

    . . . *Yaaaiiihhh*

it sounds again . . . more *piercing* still,
rising on the early summer air,
glory unleashed in ferocious timbre,
recalling bloody days of countless battles won,
thundering up to steel our marching ranks and rows . . .
death's clarion call signaling gray legions on the move,
our charge in dreadful patience inches slowly on,

vibrant with the lives of us who long to live just long enough
to lash out *lethally* once.

Mama,
in all my fourteen years, I've never seen a grander sight . . .
our division . . . great patchwork squares of *us,*
moving quiltlike across this unfamiliar land
bursting bright with summer's green,
while ever watchful on the looming heights above,
death's dark silent bores await,
gauging our inexorable approach.

Exactly when I lost my childish fright,
got over being merely *scared,*
I cannot really say,
but I've not lived this far beyond Manassas
to feel anything other than a grown man's chilling *fear,*
mingled with dear memories of you, *Mama,*
of Daddy, too,
and older brother Jake . . . *may God protect him, please* . . .
and sweet little freckle-faced Sister,
of our piney-wood home in Caroline
where honeysuckles linger softly fragrant
on barefoot summer evenings . . .

    rat-a-tat-tat . . . rat-a tat-tat

. . . the *dream* of peaceful yesterdays, I dream,
though countless tread of warrior feet surround,
some booted, many barefooted, too,
all tramping out fear's cold distillate . . .

. . . while Cory's voice lifts hoarse with fright again,
softly, sadly, saying . . .

> "When them Yankee heavy guns open up, Abner,
> they're going to give our boys pure hell. If I don't
> make it and you do, tell my mama that I love her."

Mama,
what glory making war
when all the children die.

Suddenly, *distantly,*
beyond our vast approach,
the heights all rupture fiercely . . .

smoke-puffs oddly frame a deadly hilltop line . . .
the silent guns of Cory's fear unleashed at last.
Death rains down upon our marching ranks
even before the sound arrives
to make us all aware . . .

. . . *everywhere* the earth erupts, disgorging flame,
flares roilingly with smoking dark,
hell fired by screaming shot and shell.
A mighty moan goes up,
a wail of *life.*
Beneath The Reaper's trenchant blade,
our perfect rows cut down,
reduced by human shrieks,
to cries of mortal pain.

Geyser bursts the shot and shell,
the dead leap oddly crumpled skyward,
all caught up now,
all blasted and all churning,
the flying severed parts of us
make a blinding crimson haze
tinctured shrieking raw by fear
beneath that deathly hilltop Yankee cannonade.

Stunned, we falter . . . brigades reeling,
wounded
awash in our own blood,
we *stagger* . . .
but step bravely on toward death and glory too,
just to yell once more with pride . . .

. . . *Yaaaiiihhh*

Fiercely, from our withered ranks,
above the thunder-death of guns,
the sound redounds to heaven's heights,
then back once more it rolls to earth
to touch it still un-trembling . . .

. . . *Yaaaiiihhh*

but fainter now,
much softer,
diminishing somewhat with the agony of our marching climb . . .

rat-a-tat-tat . . . rat-a-tat-tat

and still, I mark a cadenced beat . . .

rat-a-tat-tat . . . rat-a-tat-tat

sobbing softly like a man . . .
poor Cory's lost among the dying,
among the thousands dead . . .
our proud division blasted,
broken on this day . . .
a few of us march bravely on . . .

rat-a-tat-tat . . . rat-a-tat-tat

surely, this distant place,
this violent day,
this final hour here will be my very last as well . . .
until we meet again beyond all glory,
Mama, dearest,
goodbye . . .

. . . I love you so.

★ ★ ★ ★

Lee

★ ★ ★ ★

watching as Pickett attacks

3:40 P.M.

Even Traveler,
whinnying softly,
oddly restless in the moment
with me mounted securely on his back,
senses the *catastrophe* come full upon us now.

The land,
the very *air* itself broods hot with blood,
our blood,
spilled all out in vain.

Death's Angel strides through Pickett's ranks,
titanic trenchant hands pealing thunderclaps,
scything our boys down like so much wheat
blown chaff-like on the churning wind.

Far off, I see them now,
our magnificent boys,
like *something* wounded,
muttering vainly to itself,
their ranks all ravaged from those looming heights,
great gaping holes blown therein,
torn wide with each blood-thud-blasting *boom.*

Yet, still they stagger bravely on,
against all odds,
their bravery supreme,
nor will they break and run
in all the face of dying
to the implacable death of guns.

Childlike, my tears I long to shed and
cry out loudly once.
Yet, softly now,
unheard by any listening ear,
with lips of tortured silence,
I exhort them all,

pleading profoundly in my heart . . .

>   . . . *Turn back . . . turn back . . . you cannot win . . . turn back!*

One of my aides,
the voice of which I can't recall,
turns now to me and says,

>   "The boys keep bravely pushing on, General."

>   "Yes," I reply to my own eternal sadness, "may
>   God have mercy on them all" . . .

. . . and on *me* as well,
sole architect of this tragic madness.

What swirling maelstrom of the mind,
what twistedness of the thinking processes
so raged within my blinded head
that I could not see the plainly obvious?

Longstreet, ablest of all lieutenants,
strides his mount close by,
paler than death's hand.
I wonder:
who bears the greater agony in this matter,
he who knew full well the hour of tragedy soon to come
and warned so sternly against,
or *me* who never voiced a doubt?

. . . and *Pickett,*
broken on the field.
Pure warrior that he is,
what of George Pickett now?

★ ★ ★ ★

Pickett

★ ★ ★ ★

in the midst of battle

3:44 P.M.

Me?
George Pickett?
In charge of *this?*
This charnel house,
this ungodly killing place?

Not a man of them will live unscathed
throughout this holocaust,
this grimmest of our days.

Armistead has just fallen,
almost every officer down,
but still, our boys march ever on
to sting of musket,
straight toward the roar of cannon rage.

Carnage . . .
carnage unbelievable haunts our wasted lost brigades,
death unparalleled.
Were I not a man,
I would rip all rank,
tear all insignia
bodily from my form, and roll wailing in the cataclysm
of this blood-soaked earth,
this godforsaken bloodbath that I, George Pickett,
God help me,
so unknowingly made.

Yet, in perfect awe,
I view such bravery as I've never seen before.
That *far* stone wall,
a few have struggled hard to reach
where muskets flash
and bayonets slash to shine and glint
amidst the cries of wrathfulness,
to be repulsed,
or die there fighting mostly hand to hand.

My boys,
I love them all so dearly,
yet, the *end,* I sense it very near.

So be it.
Let History write of me as Death's Obliging General if it will,
but timelessly, in perfect honor too,
will it salute *their* selflessness and bravery
for ten thousand years to come.

Invincible?
No.
I cast that word upon the wind
not *us*
no *more*
not *me*
and especially not that bowed old man sitting back there on his horse . . .

. . . he who destroyed my proud division,
I no longer find the heart in me to love
due to his horrific miscalculations made
on this dreadful day so long to be remembered
for its bravery and blood.

★ ★ ★ ★

Longstreet

★ ★ ★ ★

as remnants of Pickett's attack return

3:57 P.M.

I think of those I love the most,
when duty sends them out to battle's call,
to fight
to rage
to die
to watch them writhe,
go down to fall
in blood and agony profound.

Obedient
yes
I am to a soldier's *T.*
In lockstep to its steady bugle's call, I march,
yet, truly in the end,
there dwells a greater call . . .

. . . love . . .

. . . now, count my personal agony factored by our broken fifteen thousands

. . . shredded by those booming hilltop guns,
bloodied
our boys
wasted
these countrymen I love,
mere remnants of themselves
I watch through misty eyes
the *few* unharmed *return,*
come straggling back
amongst the dying,
amongst the countless littered dead.

Now, in me grows an endless pain;
inside a deathly silence knells. . . .
God help us, I cry wordless out,
and for the obedient soldier I remained
where now only bitterest agony dwells,

I pray,
God help my tortured soul as well.

Defeat . . .
like bile, it burns,
how wide our terrible margin of it?
I ask the question duly posed,
and with my broken heart must answer . . .

    . . . we are done . . . our Cause . . . finished in this tragic hour alone.

Beside me now, astride faithful Traveler,
immobile,
ancient seeming,
timeless . . . nay . . . *immortal still,*
beyond mere *time* itself,
beautiful somehow in his tragic stillness . . .
his sad white head,
the gentled eyes
stare distantly ahead . . .

. . . now, in those distances, he says,

    "You were right all along, General, and I was so very wrong."

I start to speak but can't,
words like stones upon my stomach sit.

    "We will organize our retreat now," our commander continues quietly on.

    "I will see to it, sir," I manage softly in return.

    "Thank you, General," he then says.

    "Yes, sir," I reply.

★ ★ ★ ★

TRANSITION

★ ★ ★ ★

JULY 3, 1863

Anna Applewhite

❧ ❧ ❧ ❧

waking to a premonition—Stantonsburg, North Carolina

4:37 P.M.

My dearest sweet son, Abner . . .

I awake,
to think what utter *strangeness* here,
this *infinite* feeling within your empty room,
amongst your finite boyish things,
where memories valued gather most,
yet now,
upon this oh so fateful day,
I fear,
are spent beyond all youth as well.

Abner,
as I lay napping on your quilted bed,
a voice,
your *own,*
familiar in all its love for me,
whispered deep inside my heart . . .

　　　. . . Mama . . .

you spoke there softly, sadly, saying,
then, from someplace far away,
called out to me again . . .

　　　. . . Mama. . . .

Your *hand,* my son,
I *felt* its small caress
touch gently on my sleeping brow,
trace down my careworn face.
With perfect love,
you whispered then
one heartfelt last farewell . . .

　　　. . . Goodbye . . . sweet Mama, dearest . . . I love you so. . . . Farewell.

Sobbing softly,
I awoke,
to smell of honeysuckle
rife upon the early summer air,
life's dusky dream forever lost
among distant motes of memory
trailed off beyond despair . . .

    . . . but I will not be sad. . . .

So, let His will be done.
Not time nor eternity can disconnect
your perfect love from me.
Beyond life's great divide,
ever will I hold you in my arms again,
caress your boyish sandy head,
speak softly once your gentle loving name . . .

    . . . Abner . . .

my little child who honor called
to be a man long years before his time.
Now, Heaven waits where only angels sing . . .
farewell,
my dear sweet loving son,
until we meet again,
goodbye . . .

    . . . I'll always love you so.

                                                          ꝏ ꝏ ꝏ ꝏ

Charles Olsen

★ ★ ★ ★

field medic—Reynold's Corps

4:37 P.M.

Poor wasted little boy in gray,
all there is of you
will not be found this day
among the broken ruins
that mark this titanic killing place.

Children need feet for summer playing,
for fun and games
to romp and run on,
but one of his is off somewhere unfound.
A hole bleeds redly in his chest.

I cup his boyish sandy head,
eyes so terribly young,
so pleading out for *life* . . .
he gasps out, gurgling,
desperate beyond this final moment of himself
to consummate all time and memory
in one final whispered word . . .
blood-foamed . . . his lips strain to form it even now,
as life itself expires,
he whispers softly, sadly,
with a childlike loving smile . . .

    . . . *"Mama."*

Then, blown out to far eternity's reach,
the *spark* is gone . . .
eyes stare blankly up,
mute, unchanging,
reflecting endless skies.

I, his mortal enemy of before,
hold him briefly for the sake of youth
and no other single reason why . . .

. . . then gaze around to damn *them* all,

to damn *us* all as well,
this *raging* place,
indescribable with the horror of it all.
Relentless, the sun burns down *white* hot.
Blood soaks the trampled ground,
seas of it . . . splashes . . . blots . . . great rivulets,
seeping *tides* of infinite red,
death's *vulture* smells,
horrid exhalations,
stunning *stenches* clot the nose,
blast the eye,
the *staggered* mind,
with *shrieks* and *moanings* everywhere,
the disbelieving Blue and Gray
oddly twisted in a body-tangle of repose,
sleep in frozen pantomime,
absolved by death, by dying too,
at last, their mortal issue solved
in this warped ballet of howling mad destruction.

If not for sacrifice
and innocent blood poured out,
I would call down Heaven's Profoundest Curse
upon the heads of *those* who *truly* made
the ruination of this awful place.

But the wounded need me more right now.

I gain my feet to leave this wasted boy,
folded slightly in death's throes,
sad crumpled little child in gray . . .
drum clutched gently in one small broken hand.

THE BLUE

★ ★ ★ ★

Army of the Potomac
JULY 3, 1863

Col. Joshua Lawrence Chamberlain

★ ★ ★ ★

on the heights . . . staring down at the long valley below

5:08 A.M.

I sense it *here,*
looking down upon
the mighty struggle soon to rage
within this peaceful half-dawn place,
among these mists so churning now,
so purling softly everything in white . . .
the *rising* day redone to cannon's roar and musket's breath,
each purling bright with smoking fire,
white-hot with fiery *death.*

Distinctly,
in pre-lights semi-indistinctness,
I can see it *all,*
the conflict fast resolving,
taking shape and form,
as though time itself sweeps swift hours ahead,
clairvoyant with the struggle soon to break
in this highest of all reckonings to come.

A reckoning.
Yes,
that is the proper term . . .
these *heights,*
that gentle *valley* climbing up below,
filled up and swarming bright with sunlight-men
all bristling sharp with July's guns,
gathered for a total view of killing,
to a raging overview of blood.

If I had to wager,
and most certainly I do,
I'd say the advantage is to *us,*
blue wolf patient in his lofty lair . . .
yet our gray foes be Bengal Tigers roaring
in that moment when the battle's finally joined
and their rebel yell splits the solemn air.

Now, suddenly, just behind,
I hear a hurried trot . . .
someone . . .
an aide comes riding urgently up,
reins quickly to a pawing halt.

"Colonel, sir," he speaks formally, but clipped, "you're wanted
back at headquarters as soon as time allows."

Time?
at least enough of it to kill,
and the bitterest of all ironies is,
we don't even hate each other.

"Yes," I reply, "tell the general I'll be there as soon as time allows."

"Very good, sir," he's swift to say . . .

. . . then reins held high in both sure hands,
wheels quickly half-about to gallop on away,
as I return to pondering exactly *when,*
precisely *where,*
their greatest thrust is coming on this third
and oh so very fateful day.

★ ★ ★ ★

Gen. George Meade

★ ★ ★ ★

sitting on his cot

5:12 A.M.

My officers have quelled any thinking of retreat.

But, resigned to fight here though I am,
I do not count myself among the many
already numbered by defeat.
Yet, by virtue of my nature,
cautious
plodding
methodical at best,
they all expect the same sad fate of me.

Does this great army actually think
me born without the benefit of ears?
I've heard the rumored voices whispering . . .

> . . . *Meade? Oh yes indeed . . . he's much too cautious . . .*
> *too methodical . . . he lacks a warrior's fighting flair.*
> *Bobby Lee will break him as he's done all the others failed*
> *before . . . just you wait and see.*

Ha!
they all call me *beat* before I even start.
Yet, ever will I fool them in the end.

That old gray fox down there,
so cunning
clever
all too confident of himself,
gathering for the final stroke,
yet, soon to learn the valued lessons of the higher ground in spades.

This time the fox comes *up* to *me,*
watchful in my eagle's eyrie,
lightning leashed,
thunder poised to blast and rend,
'til failure writes not large against my warrior's name,
discontinues its blue lineage of defeat.

Cautious?
Yes, truly, I am indeed . . .
but this time,
I'm also *ready* . . .

. . . and duly aided by the rightness of *our* Cause,
and with God Almighty's help alone,
this time,
we will prevail.

★ ★ ★ ★

Maj. Gen. Winfield Hancock

★ ★ ★ ★

pondering . . . moments before penning a letter to his wife

6:30 A.M.

A stranger war, there's never been,
brother pitted against brother,
killing those you've grown to love
out of simple duty to a *Cause*.

Madness . . .
yes, it binds us *all* today,
leavened through and through by *love,*
words hurled freely out in lieu of bullets
to sanctify this tragic union,
this dance of national death we do.

Hatred . . .
would it ever set my warrior's hand more free,
were both sides driven hotly by it,
much easier would our soldier's work of slaughter,
the task of killing be.

But down there patient and abiding,
ol' Lo awaits me even now . . .
Lewis Armistead,
my best friend,
bolts of lightning raging in both hands,
to kill me if he can . . .
ol' Lo, ever faithful to the end of both of us,
of *life* itself this day.

Yet, if one of us must come to die,
to stretch our length upon this silent ground,
I'll gladly kneel before the saber's thrust
before I strike my dearest old friend down.

Father,
please,
I pray to Thee,
still our warring hands,
for blood waters this tortured land

where awful flowers grow,
with blossoms of sheer madness . . .

. . . with blooms of perfect love.

★ ★ ★ ★

Chamberlain

★ ★ ★ ★

**on the heights . . . thinking back on his top sergeant
and the battle soon to come**

7:03 A.M.

I can almost hear ol' Sergeant Kilrain now,
earthy fount of wisdom that he surely was,
in his dependable soldier's way,
survey our high position of today,
then sum up our situation well.

"Colonel, darlin'," he'd say with missing-toothy grin,
"this ground is surely lovely to defend,
and since it is, *somethin's* going to *give* today,
but it ain't going to be *our* men."

I'd smile, to nod as always,
bolstered by his confidence on the hour.

"See that they're dug in well," I'd then advise him in return.

Kilrain's eyes would glint dark pools of fire,
grin once bearlike about to growl,
then smile out more easily to explain.

"The men are dug in tight as ticks, Colonel, darlin'. So, let them
Rebs come on a-runnin' with their mighty rebel yell."

Kilrain . . .

I return from moment's reverie
to stand here gazing *far* away,
beyond the conflict of the hour,
beyond all mortals raging,
to think down deep inside the depths of me . . .

*. . . there is a love all soldiers feel quite like none other ever.
I feel it now for old Kilrain,
gentle kinsman . . .
fierce old warrior brother.*

But he was lost on yesterday,
a thousand years ago it seems,
while *now's* today,
upon these heights,
with Buster Kilrain gone, my strong right arm,
cut off, detached . . .
I feel somehow adrift,
alone,
near half our regiment's gone as well . . .

. . . yet, this ground is made to battle's order,
lovely to defend,
high
looming over all,
commanding from its crown . . .

. . . as a young lieutenant steps up to speak,

while I stand here looking down.

> "Sir," says he, "the men are ready, all positioned well.
> Word is, however, the Rebs will choose to strike
> both flanks rather than us here in the middle."

> "We'll deal with whatever comes our way," I'm swift to say.

> "Very good, sir," salutes the young lieutenant briskly,
> then off he wheels to walk away.

Yet, the question is left hanging still:
where . . . precisely will their boldest thrust yet come?
Dependent on its answer, our fate this day will turn . . .

> . . . *where will Bob Lee strike us in this most desperate of all hours?*

Personally, I think he's going to come straight at us . . .

> . . . *rampaging right up our very middle.*

★ ★ ★ ★

Jennie Wade

∽∽∽∽

Gettysburg civilian in the midst of baking

8:00 A.M.

Singing softly,
humming on this warmest day,
I do my morning's baking work,
mindful of the fact that
just beyond my tuneful strains
two mighty foes engage
to leaven this war-torn land as well.

But baking never waits.
So, Mother's dough I knead
and Father's biscuits bake,
to distant boom of guns,
to pygmy cries of men hurled out
so torrid hot on burning summer air,
their tidelike rages *surging,*
oddly muted from afar.

Beyond my window, I wonder,
who is winning on the day?
which side succeeds at committing perfect mayhem best?

Hopefully, *ours,* of course,
but what is happening to whom precisely where,
I do not know for sure . . .

. . . except to say . . .

my world goes on as usual,
routinely as before,
its simple hopes, its cares, its many duties
unbothered by the wrath of those
who cast blood-shadows down upon our peaceful land.

But suddenly,
what is *this?*
Something *light,*
a *thing* so soft, so *miniscule,*

a *bee-like-stinging*
pierces strangely through my back
and out my youthful breast.

My baking hands both stop . . . *amazed.*
I *stare* . . .
a *seepage* creeping there . . .
the flowered blouse I wear
blossoms staining brightly red,
a lonely bloom traced and slowly spreading out.

I seek to call out tearfully to my mother once,
but alas, the breath of me goes out,
the fleetingness of youth,
the light of *time* itself.

Now, sow the wind with innocence,
spill the earth with blood,
count me past,
my time is done.
Father,
I am coming,
Your sweet child, Jennie Wade,
beyond all earthly sorrow
and my own short youthful days,
to take up golden wing
and forever dwell among the endless stars . . .

   . . . where mortals dare not rage.

Nelly Mae Nicholson

eighteen years old . . . thinking back wistfully to July 2 and Jeb Stuart

9:25 A.M.

Occasionally, the boom of mighty guns
I hear thudding on the morning air,
while deep within the heart of me,
my mind returns to *yesterday* and how . . .

. . . *it was such a sight to see* . . .
to be remembered well,
and, according to Father's way of thinking,
to be roundly hated, too,
these high gallopers clad all in gray . . .

. . . *Jeb Stuart's cavalry coming up the way* . . .

up *our* road at a cadenced canter
measured by their dust plume raising on the distanced air,
gaining greater definition by the gradual moment there.

I watch *enthralled*
their column's twining vast approach,
winding on to out-of-sight,
to *never* seem to end . . .
but still, they come a-riding on,
an endless flow,
in-columned by their horseback-mounted thousands,
a quarter-mile away,
straight up our dusty road toward war's brief destiny
and to *me.*

I feel *it* then . . .
the *earth* shakes trembling to their hoof beats,
marking out their way of thunder
amidst glint and gleam of sabers there,
beneath bright banners flying
oh so brightly on the hot day July air.

Invaders, yes, they truly are indeed,
one and all,

these purposeful men in gray.
Yet, they do not seem *that* distasteful,
that terribly vicious from afar,
not even half so bad as Father always likes to say.

Fierce, perhaps . . . infinitely proud as well,
but no less can be expected of that much youth
astride war's apocalyptic steeds in this,
the highest moment of all their youthful lives.

Out front there . . . *leading,*
yes,
clearly, now, I see *him* . . .
that must be Jeb Stuart,
ferocious son of warrior gods, Father says,
spawned for battle
violence bred
mayhem's thunder child,
plume stuck jaunty in his rakish hat,
sunlight bright upon his handsome face . . .

riding . . .
boldly,
ever forward,
all of them,
Jeb Stuart heading up his men,
their winding column born to saddle and to mounts,
so close I can almost smell their lathered horses now,
riding . . .
ever onward,
almost to my farmhouse
and to *me.*

Yet, oddly now
I stand here unafraid
beside our whitewashed picket fence
holding my sweet puppy, Spot,
who leaps down suddenly from my arms
to run out barking fast
scant feet in front of Jeb Stuart's
oncoming warrior's stallion . . .

. . . Stuart, who quickly signals up a cavalry halt,
dismounts unhurried at a step,
picks up my little pup,
strides over,

hands him back to me . . .

"Ma'am," he says with boyish twinkling eyes, "you must try to forgive us
what we do here in your land . . . but we will only stay awhile. What
is your little puppy's name?"

"Spot," I speak softly to this gentled man of war. "His name is Spot "

"A fine name indeed," he says, and smiles as bright as day itself . . .

. . . then with a flourished bow,
turns swift about,
remounts his grandly rearing stallion,
and calling out for "double-time,"
their column rides on off away.

I watch it dwindle in the light
'til nothing holds the fading day
but *dust,*
and memories of a *little kindness* made
amongst the tragedy of our times.

But that was all on *yesterday,*
while far off now, I hear again
like distant rolling thunder,
the guns of July booming.

Though never will I tell it now,
not in a moment or a day,
because to do so would provoke my father's perfect rage . . .

*. . . but I hope and pray Jeb Stuart lives far beyond these tragic hours
to a very ripe old age.*

❧ ❧ ❧ ❧

William Watson

★ ★ ★ ★

surgeon—105th PA

10:00 A.M.

Laying neatly out my *healing* tools,
bright gleaming instruments of trade
. . . let's see, now . . .
is everything *ready* for the day? . . .

. . . *cutting blades?*
yes
hacking saws?
yes
my cleavers and my knives?
yes
everything's honed up sharp,
at least enough to shave . . .

      . . . *but what else am I missing here?*

hmmm?
let's see . . .

ah, yes,
left out, but now, at last, *remembered,*
to numb all horrors of remembering
once doctoring time is done,
forgetfulness contained within a bottle,
healer's instrument of first choice . . .

      . . . *my beloved demijohn!*

Surely, Hippocrates would be not so pleased that
a *healing* drink or two I take each night to hurry sleep,
but he's not *here* amidst this endless mayhem raised,
the heaping gore
the mounting piles of severed legs
the arms
the legless feet
pale un-clutching hands.

Mountains of pure human wreckage *I* have *seen*,
no sober mind withstands . . .

    . . . so be not so pleased, Hippocrates,
       if you think I give a damn!

     ★ ★ ★ ★

Bill McConnell

★ ★ ★ ★

forty-nine years old—infantryman—Chamberlain's Regiment

10:06 A.M.

Day towers brightly over all,
with great potentialities for *blood* . . .

. . . yet, behind this short stone wall,
I sit, listening careful to him speak,
to *Jake,*
my youthful friend,
this boy of barely seventeen years
explaining all
before battle's hour dawns,
of all the reasons why
he came straight up from Dixie
to choose *our* side of this.

    "I guess, Bill," he says a bit with sadness and more than
    wistful, too, "I just sorta figured it was the right thing to do."

Washington Jefferson Brown

★ ★ ★ ★

dishwasher—Sykes Corps

12:29 P.M.

Wash dis pot,
scrub dat pan,
is dis *all* they ever gonna let me do?
I done come all the way up here to fight just like a man,
not wash dese here dishes like a boy . . .

. . . *somebody,* give me a gun.
I ain't mad,
just glad to be dis *free.*
If it takes some fightin' to stay dis way,
dat's O.K. with me.
I ain't scared neither,
not one damned bit . . .

somebody,
please,
give dis here man a gun!

★ ★ ★ ★

Chamberlain

★ ★ ★ ★

as Porter Alexander's bombardment begins

1:00 P.M.

A mighty barrage! . . .

. . . no greater gathering of heavy cannon firing
has this planet ever seen . . .
as thunderclaps sustain,
the heavens *heave,*
regurgitate with smoking fire and flame . . .
a *burning* rain,
shrieks,
screaming down,
incoming!

Deluged in hot iron,
the earth bursts skyward,
churning.

★ ★ ★ ★

Bill McConnell

★ ★ ★ ★

infantryman—Chamberlain's Regiment

2:57 P.M.

Anytime *now,*
they will be *coming* . . .

> *. . . nearer, my God, to thee, nearer to thee!*
> *E'en though it be a cross that raiseth me,*
> *still all my song shall be,*
> *nearer, my God, to thee;*
> *nearer, my God, to thee, nearer to thee! . . .*

my favorite hymn prayed silently . . .

> *. . . though like the wanderer, the sun gone down,*
> *darkness be over me, my rest a stone;*
> *yet in my dreams I'd be*
> *nearer, my God, to thee,*
> *nearer, my God, to thee, nearer to thee! . . .*

★ ★ ★ ★

Jake Applewhite

★ ★ ★ ★

seventeen years old—infantryman—Chamberlain's Regiment

2:59 P.M.

A *pause* before the breaking storm
holds our position locked so deathly still,
immobilized with *waiting,*
as tension builds unbearable toward that single *instant* leashed,
yet latent with the fury soon to come.

Dug in behind this short stone wall,
we lie in wait,
our mighty thousands entrenched,
enthralled,
the sheer dead *quietness* of it all,
before footfalls thunder up the long valley far below.

Death, we are in *waiting,*
yes,
a virtual porcupine of guns where heights command,
our battle lines all bristle,
gun barrels shimmering brightly,
breathless in 10,000 sweating hands
lined up in perfect silence
grimly on these looming heights above.

Yet, still farther in the valley just away,
Death's Children also gather *now,*
great patchwork squares in ordered patient gray,
intent to sow the rising breeze,
to seed the coming storm
with war's great leveling wind
and sweep us all away.

My kinsmen down there gathered,
proud Southern folk soon to cleave my rifle's sight,
my land once
my people, too,
each one and all,
before this plotted madness made them over
into my determined foes.

But *the choice* was mine alone to make,
and so I chose up *sides* to take.
Now here I sit in *blue* and wait,
to check my shot,
my powder's dry as well,
while next to me, crusty ol' Bill McConnell says,

> "Them Rebs down there, Jake . . .
> they gonna cut our hearts right out and eat 'em
> for their supper if they can."

> "No, Bill," I reply softly with a half-intended joke,
> "just *yours* . . . providing they can digest something
> that old and tough and hard."

Ol' Bill grins wry just once,
shakes his shaggy head and nods,
stares off down the sloping way
to where those muted thousands stand
in wait upon a single order raised,
then mutters softly, prophetically to himself:

> *"This is gonna be one helluva bloody fight."*

Prophetic words still hanging bleak upon the midday air,
when bright sabers lift from far below
to flash and stab the sudden air . . .
the order raised,
the order *given,*
as far-off "smoke puffs"
. . . huge blown-out silent *Os* . . .
mark their cannon's volley
crashing down like Banshees upon our distant hilltop rows.

Coming . . .
yes, they surely are indeed,
to drumbeats playing tiny in the distance far away,
their perfect patchwork squares lockstepping forward
to measured rhythms of a tune . . .

> *rat-a-tat-tat . . . rat-a-tat-tat*

and with them too,
raging fearsome and ferocious
on the ageless summer air,
lifts up their mighty battle yell . . .

. . . Yaaaiiihhh

Yes, truly . . .
they are coming now.

★ ★ ★ ★

Hancock

★ ★ ★ ★

as Pickett's Division steps out to form just beyond the wood line

3:03 P.M.

Praise be to God,
that I stand here in this glorious hour,
and should I die upon this very day
and soul take wing to Heaven's Keep,
at least, I've lived to see such beauty on display.

Were I not their dedicated enemy,
I would cry out above the battle coming,
above the conflict soon to break . . .

> *Stop! . . . hold fire! . . . we cannot harm these bravest men*
> *and their formations of sheer beauty . . .*

a *full mile* of them extending in lined view,
in perfect order moving,
to beat of battle drums,
to pace of battle flags all grandly purling,
bright beneath the sun . . .

the *sight* . . . God help me so,
I love it . . .
so clean with order,
thrilling . . .
the absolute *beauty* of it all . . .

> "Commence firing!" I bellow out so willing . . .

while deep inside still thinking . . .

> *. . . with war, I could truly fall in love . . .*
> *if not for the necessity of killing.*

★ ★ ★ ★

Chamberlain

★ ★ ★ ★

as Pickett's Division begins its distant approach

3:04 P.M.

They are coming . . .
far below
to drumbeats playing solemn
where battle pennons wave.

A glorious sight,
their lines all drawn and closely ordered
at least one full mile across.
How many by their regimented thousands?
I cannot truly say,
except that they are coming *now*
to deal *us* death this day.

Yet, *why?*
Why do we do it?
The *killing question* posed,
and now more duly raised.
I ask it of *both* sides . . .

    what stirs the warrior's rage? . . .

provokes the wrath in *us,*
or is it wrath at all?
that clothes us here in blue,
clads them down there in gray.

Madness?
no, I do not think so overall,
though the *killing* can't be sane.

Duty   Honor   Country?
we're fond of quoting that as well.

Except for *causes* so dissimilar,
identically, we're the *same:*
Yanks and Rebs,
twin brothers of the flesh

who both love life,
or so we tend to claim . . .
who pray fervently for God's protection
when the end is fast approaching near.

Yet, where dying is the issue,
I wonder:
does God take sides?
I'll wager He does not.

For *killing* and its sake alone,
I have no explanation for Mankind
and what we do here on this day,
except to say with one broad and sad defining breath . . .

        . . . we are in love . . . yes . . . but not with life . . .

        . . . our dearest love is death!

So, here within this lofty place
duty calls me to a practiced soldier's pace,
to walk along our waiting ranks,
inspect them well.
The sun burns down, a glaring hell
where grips The Reaper's bony hand
to powder, shot, and shell,
poised now to waste the foe in each of us,
that foe who truly is . . .
ourselves.

★ ★ ★ ★

Jake Applewhite

★ ★ ★ ★

infantryman—Chamberlain's Regiment

3:46 P.M.

Firing . . .
I am steady firing
'til my musket barrel burns hot.

Yet, grimly swearing one and all,
they still come tramping on.
Once, a great tide roaring,
to less than ebb tide now, they fall,
a mere seepage of themselves,
their valiant charge
laps redly on our granite shores . . .
gray flotsam vainly broken on its human self,
yet so terribly glorious by the ordered thousands
a few short hours ago.

Of their blood-mad howling swarm,
scant few remain intact . . .
yet still they pace so proudly on,
fierce eyed,
hot with curses, firing,
to certain death and dying,
they stagger bravely on.

I shoot until my finger's numb,
my smoking bore takes every darkening form in sight . . .

. . . but *look* . . .
out *there* . . .
approaching closely *now* . . .
that little drummer boy in gray . . .
how *sad* . . .
bright tears streak down his boyish face,
his cap is off somewhere,
gone from his sandy little head . . .

        . . . *Dear God . . . please. . . . Nooo!*

My recognizing cry's hurled all too late.
Beside me, ol' Bill McConnell takes fair aim,
and unknowing while cursing steady hot,
puts a single bullet straight through Abner,
my *own* small brother's gray-clad boyish heart.

Jake Applewhite

★ ★ ★ ★

infantryman—Chamberlain's Regiment

3:48 P.M.

Continuous . . .

. . . I fire on this day
in aftermaths less touched by carnage and by blood,
than in remembrance of Mama's fateful words
back home in Caroline explaining,

> "Son, let your *heart* do all the *choosing,*
> and you won't never have to answer to no man,
> 'cept yourself come Judgment Day."

And so I rightly chose *my side* of this,
this tragic place,
this *moment* here,
according to my own best careful judgments made . . .

but Father,
please,
tell little Abner that I'll always love him still,
and just for me,
as well as him whose youth poured out can never age,
let him weep not amongst the angels singing . . .

> *. . . where mortals dare not rage.*

★ ★ ★ ★

Hancock

★ ★ ★ ★

as Pickett's men cede the field in defeat

3:58 P.M.

And now they go . . .

like mist to fade
returning,
to slowly slip away,
their long gray line
once proud with banners
bloodied,
forever ended on this day.

Close by, a young lieutenant, wounded,
looks up . . . then down the way and says,

"I will tell my grandchildren about what happened here today."

"Both sides fought well . . . with honor," I nod, reply to say,

yet, all the while still thinking . . .

. . . those boys in gray . . . not once in all my warrior's life
have I seen such incredible bravery on display.

★ ★ ★ ★

Jake Applewhite

★ ★ ★ ★

infantryman—Chamberlain's Regiment

4:48 P.M.

The guns all stilled . . .

. . . yet, here I lie still half-*amazed*
to feel this *needless* little hole in me . . .
un-hurtful, yes,
yet so *deathly* trickling there in red.

A *tiny* flow,
these minutes of my days
bleed out the gradual life of me.
I mark them timed in seconds now
'til Death's repose takes up my soul,
sets my earthly clay so free . . .

dying . . .
sweet dreams of life
of peace
of love
of home once more again
to grow the gentled earth with bursting green
and children too,
alas . . .

> *no more . . . no more . . .*
> *all ended by a bayonet's trenchant sheen . . .*

. . . yet, *he* who opened up Death's Door for me,
I did the *same* for *him.*

Now, side by side,
spread eagle near to touch,
we bleed the broken earth
'neath blazing sun,
eyes up to Heaven's Gate . . .
'til by my ear, so softly now,
his Rebel's voice speaks quietly there,
childlike,

without *hate* . . .

"I am so very sorry," he whispers near, yet somehow far away.

"I am, too," I say . . .

to *fade,*
to grow so silent then . . .
one final smile
by Grace is *stilled*
as life's brief window shuts.

Beyond its far bright sill,
eternity waits . . .
for each of us . . .

. . .*forever*

★ ★ ★ ★

RETREAT

★ ★ ★ ★

JULY 4, 1863

Chamberlain

★ ★ ★ ★

on the heights . . . as the Army of Northern Virginia begins its long march southward

9:00 A.M.

Thank God,
they leave;
once broken, now they *go.*
Yes!
defeated . . .

. . . down there so very far below,
their sounds all unmistakable,
by distance softly *muffled,*
to creak of cannon moan,
to tread of leaden feet,
gray legions steady marching,
moving out now in retreat.

To have fought so well,
so nobly,
what must they be *feeling* now? . . .

. . . perhaps that which we
who sit in victory's lofty seat
have known so very well ourselves . . .

. . . a terrible *hollowness* within,
a *great blood-swept howling darkness*
tolling out the immeasurable horror of it all,
of battle's *doom* remembered,
nay, *relived,*
of life and limb all wasted,
of men torn puppetlike asunder,
so uselessly expended . . .

defeat
as bitter
black as sin
bereft of sons
stepchild with no human brothers . . .

unloved
retreat declares itself *alone*
heartsick
the ultimate in all emptiness
the epitome of all leaving
toward emptiness, they go . . .

> *. . . which is precisely why we should mass within the hour*
> *and strike them now a mortal killing blow!*

Lee

★ ★ ★ ★

astride his beloved Traveler

4:00 P.M.

Raining . . .
the army dissolving grayly up ahead,
trekking
weary through the falling wet,
through the mists of rising time.

I *ride*
amongst the muddy creak of cannon's groan,
to sodden slogging steps of men,
to mud's deep sucking pull on hooves,
. . . chest hurts a lot . . .
yet, to cast no blame at all,
except on *me* alone.

But still, I fall to wondering:
is there not in all of nature somewhere
a creature who *feeds* upon itself,
whose awful consumption is its own brief life and limb?

> *Jackson,*
> *our strong stonewall,*
> *killed . . .*
> *consumed by our own men . . .*

. . . those Carolina boys,
fiercer than 10,000 mountain lions . . .
yet, for the accident of a single errant bullet aimed,
we'd have owned the higher ground
and victory in these final hours of our days.

But off such tiny incidents unrevealed
until the moment finally turns,
does the fate of nations oft depend.

Traveler, my old beloved friend,
I tell you truly, there is nothing more dismal than retreat.

I wish this rain would end.

AFTERMATH

★ ★ ★ ★

APRIL 9, 1865

Lee

★ ★ ★ ★

Appomattox Courthouse

12:30 P.M.

Grant . . .

    a simple decency in this man,
    a tendency in his patient stillness
    to accept this final moment here
    as an *ending* to it all . . .

. . . no *conditions* offered
nor forgiveness rendered of our Cause,
his final terms appeal to none of that,
yet, respectfully, we've closed this day with honor . . .

    . . . both sides have fought like men.

A clock ticks quietly over all
recording time for history's sake.
We stand to shake.
His eyes hold mine and mine to his.
I turn to leave,
outside, to mount and slowly ride away . . .

. . . far from War's soul-blasting bleakness
as gaunt as ancient bones,
omnipresent as The Reaper's pall . . .
long years have made this brooding emptiness in me,
each tug and sway indentured to its exigencies,
to its terrible beck and call.

Slowly on beneath this springtime day,
I ride . . .
these boys in blue all line the way,
some missing arms, some lacking feet,
but gentled now from raging,
respectful in a sadly smiling way,
where Traveler's cadenced hoof-steps
mark a solemn passing beat.

Somewhere off . . . somewhere away,
a band tunes up with "Dixie"
playing softly on the fragrant air.
Odd, these boys, I sense them
clad all so brightly here in blue,
belong once more with me,
and I, once more, with them . . .

> *my countrymen again,*
> *a nation binding in repair,*
> *healing its deep wounds.*

I ride on off into the sun
neither diminished by the distance
nor gaining by the moment here.
Of *history* itself . . . surely it will have its way with me.
Yet to its careful scribes, I say:
so be it.

A small blue butterfly lights suddenly on Traveler's ear;
one small flick and off it lifts to fly away.
My eyes follow upward with a weary smile.
Odd, I've not seen *one* since this tragic *thing* began,
nor a single chirping bird,
nor even a child's bright happy smile,
not *anything* at all,
beyond these endless leagues of death
that mark my grimmest days.

Riding on beneath grandfather trees,
beneath the dappled light,
beyond the annals of all time itself,
I lean over,
pat Traveler's shoulder affectionately once,
whispering quietly on the spring-filled air,

> "We won't have to ride this way again, old friend," I say. "No, not us.
> We're going home at last. Thank God, it's finally at an end."

Yes,
going home to loved ones now,
to friends,
to my family . . .

> *. . . and to life*

★ ★ ★ ★

Grant

★ ★ ★ ★

Appomattox Courthouse

12:30 P.M.

Lee . . .

I did not imagine him
this old . . .
white headed,
grandfatherly even,
clad formally in gray . . .
nor so terribly *still,*
eyes so bright,
so deeply sad,
as though The Creator Himself has forged within them both a cosmic pain . . .

. . . nor even half so wearied by his Cause
now folded back upon itself,
broken abysmally in defeat.

Abysmal?
no, strike that word . . .
to him, it does not apply,
nor to anything of his,
nor has it place at this final meeting here.

I see him sitting there quite tangibly,
quite human and quite *real,*
yet, as though to *disappear* from the moment balanced
and reassume his rightful place among
the gentler more watchful gods.

Somewhere, a clock ticks softly over all
recording time for history's sake . . .
yet, upon him now, its careful flow
makes no trace at all,
does not seem to touch or even hold him in the hour,
as though it parts respectfully to move around
like a pebble in a stream.

Yet, as two commanders,

we have faced each other on this day,
talking of it all . . .
now the formalities of our business here are done.

His hand extends . . .
we shake as *men.*

"Goodbye, General," he speaks formally in farewell.

"Goodbye, General," I speak quietly and the same.

Though tired, his grip is firm,
a *warrior's* hand . . .
he stands,
to rise up slowly now,
his height unfolding by degrees,
not broken by defeat,
but momentary there
among dust motes slanting *golden* in the room . . .
his countenance beatifically sad,
solemn as the hour sealed,
a warrior's face,
come down to terms with all the horrors of the past,
at rest,
at *peace* at last.

"I think I will be going home now," he says with simple dignity.

And thus, about, he turns to go.
I follow not too far behind.

Outside, he mounts,
salutes me once, as I do him . . .
then lifting reins,
turns to ride away . . .

> *. . . time will never hold him in this place, I am thinking as he goes.*
> *No, not him. Beyond this hour and this moment here, he will be*
> *remembered as far more than just a man.*

Our boys in blue who line his passing way
sense this in their soldier's way as well,
the timelessness of him who rides on slowly now between
their ordered ranks,
on down their ordered rows.

Somewhere off . . . somewhere away,
a band tunes up with "Dixie"
playing softly on the fragrant air.
He touches once his warrior's hat,
grateful of this final tribute made.

I watch him go.
I who fought him in the name of *every* man.
I who am *every* man in most particular ways,
ordinary, yes,
so plodding in my shuffling gait,
just plain old ordinary *me* . . .
yet in him, there rides away *a god* . . .
though still . . .

   . . . I do not envy him the remainder of his days.

★ ★ ★ ★

REQUIEM

★ ★ ★ ★

Amongst Immortals

★ ★ ★ ★

All life is lived, all time is done,
no memory lingers here
beneath this gentle earth
so rife with springtime sun.
We sleep forever and unknowing
of this hallowed ground we made.
On battlefields of honor, our youth poured out,
played out in violent days.
One instant there amongst immortals raging,
something darkened out our sun.
Now all is quiet, so solemn here
where weathered stones inscribe our names,
where once our race was run.

All life is lived, all time is done.
We sleep forever now with angels
who sing of glory and of sacred honor won,
of life and time that's never done
as long as one true heart remembers us . . .

    . . . this land's most valiant sons.

★ ★ ★ ★

ACKNOWLEDGMENTS

★ ★ ★ ★

It is with the deepest sense of appreciation that the author wishes to thank the following people for their help: Danny Hooks, Patsy Ferrell, Betsy Barber Bancroft, James Everett Kibler, Celia Batchelor, Teri Kennedy, Hope Young, Lee S. Gliarmis, Jim and Mary Claire Bilbro, Duane and Ann Creech, Alexander Moore, E. Sherwood Bridges, Gail Roberson, Elizabeth Whitley Roberson.

Special thanks to Steve Phillips for setting up my Web site.